The Real Estate Success Blueprint: Mastering Strategies and Building Wealth

Chapter 1: Introduction to Real Estate Mastery

- Introduction to the importance of mastering real estate strategies.
- Overview of what readers will learn.
- Brief anecdotes or success stories to inspire readers.

Chapter 2: The Real Estate Mindset

- The importance of a growth mindset in real estate.
- Overcoming common mental barriers.
- Developing resilience and adaptability.

Chapter 3: Building Your Real Estate Knowledge Base

- Key concepts and terminology in real estate.
- Essential resources for continuous learning.
- The role of mentors and networking.

Chapter 4: Identifying Investment Opportunities

- How to spot lucrative real estate deals.
- Analyzing markets and trends.
- Using data and tools to evaluate potential investments.

Chapter 5: Financing Your Real Estate Investments

- Understanding different financing options.
- Strategies for securing funding.
- Managing finances to maximize returns.

Chapter 6: Negotiation Mastery

- The art of negotiation in real estate.
- Key phrases and tactics to use.
- Real-life negotiation scenarios and outcomes.

Chapter 7: Building and Managing a Real Estate Portfolio

- Diversifying your investments.

- Long-term vs. short-term investments.
- Effective portfolio management strategies.

Chapter 8: Marketing Your Properties

- Effective marketing strategies for selling or renting properties.
- Utilizing digital marketing tools and social media.
- Creating compelling property listings.

Chapter 9: Legal and Regulatory Considerations

- Understanding real estate laws and regulations.
- Navigating contracts and agreements.
- Mitigating risks and avoiding legal pitfalls.

Chapter 10: Scaling Your Real Estate Business

- Strategies for growing your real estate business.
- Leveraging technology and automation.
- Building a team and delegating tasks.

Chapter 11: Real Estate Investment Strategies for Beginners

- Introduction to various investment strategies.
- Case studies of successful beginner investors.
- Step-by-step guide to your first investment.

Chapter 12: Advanced Investment Techniques

- Exploring advanced investment strategies.
- Detailed case studies of high-level investments.
- Risk management and maximizing returns.

Chapter 13: Maintaining and Enhancing Property Value

- Best practices for property maintenance.
- Upgrading properties to increase value.
- Sustainability and green initiatives in real estate.

Chapter 14: The Future of Real Estate

- Emerging trends and technologies in real estate.

- Adapting to changes in the market.
- Future-proofing your real estate investments.

Chapter 15: Conclusion and Next Steps

- Recap of key takeaways.
- Actionable steps for readers to implement.
- Encouragement and motivation for ongoing success.

Chapter 1: **Introduction to Real Estate Mastery**

Welcome to "The Real Estate Success Blueprint: Mastering Strategies and Building Wealth," a comprehensive guide crafted for both seasoned investors and newcomers to the dynamic world of real estate. In this book, we embark on a journey that transcends mere property transactions, diving deep into the strategies and mindsets that foster enduring success in real estate investing.

Why Real Estate?

Real estate stands as an enduring pillar of wealth creation, distinguished by its tangible assets, potential for appreciation, passive income streams, and unique tax advantages. Unlike other forms of investment, real estate offers the compelling advantage of leveraging other people's money (OPM), allowing investors to magnify their returns and build substantial wealth over time.

The Real Estate Mastery Framework

Central to our exploration is the Real Estate Mastery Framework, an integrated approach designed to empower you with the knowledge and strategies necessary for navigating and thriving in the real estate landscape.

1. Mindset

The foundation of success in real estate begins with mindset. We delve into the importance of cultivating a growth mindset, which enables investors to embrace challenges as opportunities for growth. Overcoming mental barriers, developing resilience, and fostering adaptability are pivotal to navigating the inevitable highs and lows of real estate investing.

2. Knowledge

Knowledge serves as the cornerstone of informed decision-making in real estate. We equip you with essential concepts, resources, and strategies essential for success. From understanding market trends and financial analysis to leveraging technological advancements and building a robust network of mentors and industry professionals, continuous learning becomes the bedrock of your journey.

3. Action

Taking strategic action is paramount. We guide you through every stage of the investment lifecycle: identifying lucrative opportunities, securing financing through traditional and creative means, mastering negotiation techniques, meticulously managing your portfolio, implementing effective marketing strategies, navigating legal considerations, and scaling your real estate business for sustainable growth.

Inspiration from Success Stories

Throughout this book, we draw inspiration from real-life success stories and case studies of exemplary real estate investors. These narratives not only illustrate the principles discussed but also provide practical insights and actionable strategies that you can integrate into your own investment strategy.

Conclusion

In "The Real Estate Success Blueprint," we embark on a transformative journey together—one fueled by knowledge, guided by strategic action, and fortified by a resilient mindset. Whether you aspire to build a diverse portfolio of properties, generate passive income streams, or achieve financial independence through real estate, this book equips you with the tools and insights to turn your aspirations into reality.

Chapter 2: **The Real Estate Mindset**

Success in real estate investing hinges on more than just financial acumen; it begins with cultivating the right mindset. A growth mindset, popularized by psychologist Carol Dweck, emphasizes the belief that abilities and intelligence can be developed through dedication and hard work. In the realm of real estate, this means fostering a belief in your capacity to learn, grow, and overcome challenges through persistence and continuous improvement.

Overcoming Mental Barriers

Many aspiring real estate investors encounter formidable mental barriers that can impede progress and success. These barriers include fear of failure, self-doubt, and analysis paralysis—the inability to make decisions due to overthinking. Overcoming these challenges requires intentional strategies:

1. Embrace Failure as a Learning Opportunity

Instead of viewing failure as a setback, embrace it as a stepping stone to success. Each setback presents valuable lessons that can refine your strategies and enhance your expertise. By reframing failure as a necessary part of the learning process, you empower yourself to persist despite obstacles.

2. Build Confidence through Education and Action

Confidence in real estate investing stems from knowledge and experience. Continuously educate yourself about market trends, investment strategies, and financial analysis. Start with small, manageable investments to build competence and confidence gradually. As you accumulate successes, your confidence will naturally grow, enabling you to tackle larger and more complex investment opportunities.

3. Take Action to Overcome Analysis Paralysis

Analysis paralysis can be debilitating for investors, preventing them from seizing opportunities due to excessive analysis and indecision. Combat this by taking decisive action, even if it starts with modest steps. Begin by researching potential properties, analyzing their investment potential, and making informed decisions based on your findings. Action not only breaks the cycle of indecision but also propels you forward on your investment journey.

Developing Resilience and Adaptability

The real estate market is inherently volatile and subject to fluctuating economic conditions, regulatory changes, and evolving consumer preferences. To thrive in this dynamic environment, cultivate resilience and adaptability:

1. Stay Informed and Agile

Stay abreast of market trends, economic indicators, and regulatory developments that impact the real estate sector. Continuous learning and information gathering equip you to anticipate changes and make informed investment decisions. Being proactive rather than reactive allows you to capitalize on emerging opportunities and mitigate potential risks.

2. Leverage Networking for Insights and Support

Build a robust network of industry professionals, mentors, and fellow investors who can offer diverse perspectives, guidance, and potential partnerships. Networking not only expands your knowledge base but also provides access to valuable resources, investment opportunities, and moral support during challenging times.

3. Reflect, Adjust, and Evolve

Regularly assess your investment strategies, outcomes, and lessons learned from both successes and setbacks. Reflective practice enables you to identify patterns of success, areas for improvement, and adjustments needed to align with changing market conditions. Flexibility in adapting your strategies based on empirical data and market feedback enhances your ability to achieve sustained success in real estate investing.

Visualization and Goal Setting

Harnessing the power of visualization and setting actionable goals is crucial for translating aspirations into tangible achievements in real estate investing:

1. Visualize Success and Maintain Focus

Allocate dedicated time each day to visualize your long-term success in real estate. Visualize yourself achieving significant milestones, closing lucrative deals, and expanding your investment portfolio. Visualization enhances motivation, reinforces commitment to your goals, and cultivates a positive mindset conducive to achieving success.

2. Set SMART Goals for Clarity and Accountability

Effective goal setting involves creating SMART goals—Specific, Measurable, Achievable, Relevant, and Time-bound. Break down your overarching investment objectives into smaller, manageable milestones with clear deadlines. For instance, set specific targets for acquiring properties, generating rental income, achieving a certain return on investment (ROI), or diversifying your portfolio across different asset classes.

3. Review and Adjust Goals Regularly

Periodically review your progress towards achieving your goals, adjusting timelines or strategies as necessary to stay on track. Celebrate achievements, learn from setbacks, and refine your goals based on evolving market conditions and personal priorities. Adapting your goals ensures they remain relevant, realistic, and aligned with your long-term vision for financial success through real estate investing.

Chapter 3: Building Your Real Estate Knowledge Base

To succeed in real estate investing, it's crucial to grasp fundamental concepts and terminology that underpin the industry. Here are some essential terms every investor should know:

1. Equity

Equity in real estate refers to the difference between the market value of a property and the outstanding balance on any mortgages or loans secured against it. It represents the owner's stake in the property's value.

2. Cap Rate (Capitalization Rate)

The cap rate is a measure used to evaluate the potential return on investment (ROI) of a property. It is calculated by dividing the property's net operating income (NOI) by its current market value or purchase price. A higher cap rate generally indicates a higher potential return relative to the property's price.

3. Cash Flow

Cash flow in real estate refers to the net income generated from a property after deducting all operating expenses and mortgage payments. Positive cash flow indicates that the property generates more income than it costs to maintain and finance.

4. Appreciation

Appreciation refers to the increase in the value of a property over time due to various factors such as market demand, inflation, and property improvements. Real estate investors often seek properties in areas expected to experience significant appreciation.

5. Leverage

Leverage involves using borrowed funds, such as mortgages or loans, to finance a real estate investment. By leveraging other people's money (OPM), investors can potentially amplify their returns, as long as the property's return on investment exceeds the cost of borrowing.

Essential Resources for Continuous Learning

Real estate is a dynamic and evolving field, making continuous learning essential for staying informed and competitive. Here are valuable resources to expand your knowledge:

1. Books

Books authored by successful investors and industry experts provide in-depth insights and strategies for real estate investing. Recommended titles include classics like "Rich Dad Poor Dad" by Robert Kiyosaki and practical guides like "The Book on Rental Property Investing" by Brandon Turner.

2. Podcasts

Real estate podcasts offer convenient access to expert advice, market insights, and success stories from seasoned investors. Popular podcasts such as "BiggerPockets Real Estate Podcast" and "The Real Estate Guys Radio Show" feature interviews with industry leaders and actionable tips for investors at all levels.

3. Online Courses and Webinars

Platforms like Udemy, Coursera, and BiggerPockets offer a plethora of online courses and webinars tailored to various aspects of real estate investing. These courses cover topics ranging from property analysis and financing strategies to property management and market trends.

4. Industry Publications

Subscribing to industry publications such as "Real Estate Investor Magazine" and "Forbes Real Estate Council" provides access to the latest news, trends, and expert opinions shaping the real estate market. These publications offer valuable insights into market dynamics, investment strategies, and regulatory changes affecting investors.

The Role of Mentors and Networking in Real Estate

Building relationships with mentors and expanding your professional network are invaluable assets in your journey as a real estate investor:

1. Finding a Mentor

A mentorship with an experienced investor or industry professional can provide personalized guidance, practical advice, and invaluable insights gleaned from years of hands-on experience. Seek mentors through real estate events, local investor groups, and online forums where seasoned professionals actively engage.

2. Building a Network

Networking is a cornerstone of success in real estate investing, offering opportunities to discover deals, forge partnerships, and exchange knowledge with peers. Attend industry conferences, join real estate associations such as the National Association of Realtors (NAR), and participate in online communities like LinkedIn groups focused on real estate investing.

3. Leveraging Relationships

Nurture relationships with mentors and network contacts by offering value, staying informed about industry developments, and seeking advice regularly. Maintain open communication channels to leverage their expertise, gain referrals, and access new investment opportunities that align with your investment goals.

Chapter 4: **Identifying Investment Opportunities**

Successful real estate investing hinges on the ability to identify and capitalize on profitable opportunities. Here are critical factors to evaluate when assessing potential investments:

1. Location

Location is paramount in real estate investing as it significantly influences property value, rental demand, and potential for appreciation. Factors to consider include:

Job Growth: Areas with strong job markets tend to attract more residents and drive housing demand.
School Quality: Properties in proximity to high-performing schools often command higher prices and rental rates.

Safety and Amenities: Low crime rates and desirable amenities such as parks, shopping centers, and public transportation enhance property desirability.

Investing in well-located properties mitigates risks and increases the likelihood of long-term value appreciation.

2. Market Trends

Analyzing local market trends provides insights into current and future investment opportunities:

Property Price Movements: Track changes in property prices over time to identify trends and market cycles.

Rental Rates: Assess rental rates in the area to gauge potential rental income and cash flow.

Inventory Levels: Low inventory coupled with high demand typically leads to competitive markets and price appreciation.

Understanding these dynamics helps investors navigate market fluctuations and make informed decisions.

3. Property Condition

Evaluate the condition of prospective properties to assess investment feasibility and potential renovation costs:

Repairs and Renovations: Properties requiring repairs or updates may offer value-add opportunities but require careful cost-benefit analysis.

Structural Integrity: Ensure the property meets safety and regulatory standards to avoid costly surprises post-purchase.

Long-Term Maintenance: Consider ongoing maintenance costs to sustain property value and tenant satisfaction.

Thorough property inspections and assessments are crucial for estimating total investment costs and potential returns.

Analyzing Markets and Trends

Effective market analysis involves evaluating economic indicators, supply and demand dynamics, comparable sales, and rental market conditions:

1. Economic Indicators

Monitor key economic indicators to gauge market health and potential for real estate investment:

Employment Rates: Strong job growth correlates with increased housing demand and rental occupancy.
Population Growth: Growing populations indicate expanding housing needs and potential for property appreciation.
GDP Growth: Economic growth stimulates real estate activity and supports property value stability.
Understanding these factors helps predict market trends and investment opportunities.

2. Supply and Demand Dynamics

Assess supply and demand dynamics to identify areas with favorable market conditions:

High Demand, Low Supply: Markets with limited housing inventory relative to demand often experience price appreciation and competitive rental markets.
Vacancy Rates: Low vacancy rates suggest strong rental demand and potential for stable cash flow.
Balancing supply and demand dynamics optimizes investment strategy and mitigates market risks.

3. Comparable Sales (Comps)

Analyze recent sales of similar properties (comps) to determine fair market value and pricing benchmarks:

Property Comparisons: Evaluate size, location, condition, and amenities of comparable properties to estimate market value.
Sales Trends: Track trends in sales prices and time on market to assess market competitiveness and pricing strategies.
Using comps facilitates accurate property valuation and enhances negotiation leverage.

4. Rental Market Analysis

For investors targeting rental properties, comprehensive rental market analysis provides critical insights:

Rental Rates: Determine prevailing rental rates for comparable properties to estimate potential rental income.
Vacancy Rates: Low vacancy rates indicate strong rental demand and occupancy stability.

Tenant Demographics: Understand tenant preferences and demographics to tailor property features and marketing strategies.

Analyzing the rental market optimizes rental income projections and informs property management strategies.

Using Data and Tools to Evaluate Investments

Harnessing data-driven insights and specialized tools enhances investment decision-making and portfolio management:

1. Real Estate Websites

Explore platforms like Zillow, Redfin, and Realtor.com for property listings, market trends, and historical sales data:

Property Research: Access detailed property information, photos, and virtual tours to evaluate investment potential.

Market Insights: Review neighborhood profiles, school ratings, crime statistics, and amenities to assess location suitability.

Real estate websites provide comprehensive resources for initial investment research and property comparisons.

2. Real Estate Investment Software

Utilize specialized software tools to streamline property analysis, financial modeling, and investment planning:

ROI Calculation: Use software like Mashvisor, RealData, and DealCheck to calculate ROI, analyze cash flow projections, and assess investment risks.

Scenario Planning: Conduct scenario analyses to evaluate different investment strategies, financing options, and market conditions.

Investment software enhances decision-making accuracy and facilitates strategic portfolio management.

3. Market Reports

Access market reports from real estate firms, local government agencies, and industry associations for in-depth market analysis and strategic insights:

Market Trends: Review comprehensive reports on economic indicators, housing market trends, and regulatory changes impacting real estate.

Expert Analysis: Gain perspectives from industry experts and market analysts on emerging trends, investment opportunities, and risk factors.

Market reports provide authoritative data and expert commentary to support informed investment decisions.

Chapter 5: **Financing Your Real Estate Investments**

Securing financing is a pivotal step in real estate investing, offering access to capital for property acquisitions, renovations, and portfolio expansion. Understanding various financing options and implementing effective strategies can enhance your ability to fund investment opportunities.

Common Financing Options

Conventional Loans:
Conventional loans are traditional mortgage products offered by banks and credit unions. These loans typically require a down payment of at least 20% and adhere to strict qualification criteria regarding credit scores, income verification, and debt-to-income ratios.

FHA Loans:
Insured by the Federal Housing Administration (FHA), these loans are designed to assist first-time homebuyers and individuals with limited financial resources. FHA loans offer more flexible qualification criteria, including lower down payments (as low as 3.5%) and competitive interest rates compared to conventional loans.

Hard Money Loans:
Hard money loans are short-term financing solutions provided by private lenders or investors. These loans are commonly used for fix-and-flip projects or investments requiring quick access to capital. They typically feature higher interest rates and shorter repayment terms, reflecting the higher risk associated with these types of loans.

Private Money Loans:
Private money loans involve borrowing from individuals or private investors rather than traditional financial institutions. These loans offer flexible terms and faster approval processes but may come with higher interest rates and fees. Private money lenders often base their decisions on the property's potential and the borrower's track record.

Seller Financing:
In a seller financing arrangement, the property seller acts as the lender, providing financing to the buyer. This option can offer flexible terms, lower upfront costs, and streamlined approval processes compared to traditional loans. Seller financing is particularly beneficial when conventional financing is challenging to obtain or for unique property transactions.

Strategies for Securing Funding

Securing financing for real estate investments requires proactive strategies to enhance creditworthiness and establish strong relationships with lenders:

Improve Your Credit Score:
Strengthen your credit profile by paying down debts, making timely payments, and avoiding new credit applications before seeking financing. A higher credit score improves your eligibility for favorable loan terms and lower interest rates.

Save for a Down Payment:
Accumulate savings to increase your down payment, ideally aiming for at least 20% of the property's purchase price. A larger down payment reduces the loan-to-value ratio, potentially lowering monthly mortgage payments and improving loan approval chances.

Build Relationships with Lenders:
Cultivate relationships with local banks, credit unions, and private lenders. Attend networking events, establish regular communication, and demonstrate reliability to enhance trust and increase access to competitive financing options.

Leverage Partnerships:
Collaborate with other investors or partners to pool resources and secure funding for larger or more complex investment opportunities. Partnerships can provide access to additional capital, diversified expertise, and shared financial responsibilities, strengthening overall investment strategies.

Managing Finances to Maximize Returns

Effective financial management is essential for optimizing returns and sustaining long-term profitability in real estate investing:

Create a Detailed Budget:

Develop comprehensive budgets for each property investment, encompassing acquisition costs, renovation expenses, ongoing operational costs, and contingencies for unforeseen repairs or vacancies. A well-defined budget helps you monitor expenses and maintain financial discipline throughout the investment lifecycle.

Monitor Cash Flow Regularly:
Track rental income, operating expenses, and cash flow performance diligently. Positive cash flow is crucial for covering mortgage payments, property maintenance, and generating passive income. Use financial management tools or software to streamline cash flow analysis and ensure financial stability.

Plan for Unexpected Costs:
Establish an emergency fund to address unexpected expenses such as major repairs, prolonged vacancies, or economic downturns impacting rental income. Maintaining adequate reserves safeguards your investments and minimizes financial strain during challenging periods.

Refinance and Reinvest Profits:
Periodically evaluate refinancing options to capitalize on lower interest rates or access equity accumulated in properties. Refinancing can lower monthly payments, improve cash flow, or provide funds for reinvestment in additional properties or portfolio enhancements, accelerating wealth accumulation.

Chapter 6: **Negotiation Mastery**

Negotiation is a fundamental skill in real estate investing, influencing deal outcomes, profitability, and relationships with counterparties. Mastering the art of negotiation requires understanding key principles, employing effective strategies, and learning from practical scenarios.

Key Principles of Successful Negotiation

Successful negotiation hinges on several foundational principles that guide effective communication and strategy development:

Preparation:
Thoroughly research the property, market conditions, and the motivations of the other party before entering negotiations. Preparation provides critical insights and enhances confidence, enabling informed decision-making and strategic positioning.

Active Listening:
Engage in active listening to understand the other party's needs, concerns, and objectives. Listening attentively fosters rapport, builds trust, and uncovers valuable information that can be leveraged during negotiations to achieve mutually beneficial outcomes.

Flexibility:
Remain flexible throughout negotiations, willing to adapt strategies and explore creative solutions that address both parties' interests. Flexibility increases the likelihood of reaching agreements that satisfy diverse needs and preferences, fostering long-term relationships and repeat business opportunities.

Key Phrases and Tactics to Enhance Negotiation

Effective negotiation relies on employing strategic phrases and tactics that enhance leverage and influence:

Anchoring:
Initiate negotiations with a strategically positioned offer or anchor point that sets expectations and frames subsequent discussions. Anchoring influences the other party's perception of value and establishes a reference point for further negotiations.

Silence:
Utilize silence strategically during negotiations to prompt the other party to divulge information, reconsider their position, or make concessions. Silence creates psychological pressure and encourages dialogue, facilitating progress towards mutually acceptable agreements.

Conditional Offers:
Present conditional offers that incorporate specific contingencies or requirements, such as timelines or additional terms. For instance, "I'm prepared to offer $X if we can finalize the agreement within 30 days." Conditional offers clarify expectations and facilitate negotiation progress while protecting your interests.

Framing:
Frame offers and counteroffers positively to emphasize benefits and fairness. Instead of outright rejection, reframe proposals in terms of market comparables or prevailing conditions to maintain constructive dialogue and explore alternative solutions.

Real-Life Negotiation Scenarios and Outcomes

Learning from practical negotiation scenarios illustrates application of strategies and principles in real estate transactions:

Scenario 1: Negotiating a Purchase Price

Situation: A buyer identifies a property for investment and initiates negotiations with the seller.

Strategy: The buyer conducts thorough research on comparable property sales (comps) and highlights necessary repairs or upgrades required. They anchor negotiations with a competitive initial offer based on market analysis.

Outcome: The seller initially counters with a higher price, citing recent market trends. However, leveraging comps and emphasizing the property's condition, the buyer successfully negotiates a reduced purchase price, achieving a favorable deal.

Scenario 2: Renegotiating After an Inspection

Situation: During property inspection, the buyer uncovers significant structural issues that were not disclosed.

Strategy: The buyer engages the seller to renegotiate terms, proposing either repairs to address identified issues or a price reduction reflective of repair costs and reduced property value.

Outcome: Recognizing the validity of the inspection findings and the buyer's proposal, the seller agrees to a price reduction. The renegotiated terms accommodate necessary repairs and align with updated property valuation, allowing the transaction to proceed with mutual satisfaction.

Scenario 3: Negotiating Lease Terms

Situation: A landlord seeks to secure a long-term tenant for a commercial property.

Strategy: The landlord conducts a needs assessment with prospective tenants, understanding their business requirements and preferences for lease terms. They propose flexible lease options tailored to tenant needs, including incentives for extended lease durations or customization allowances.

Outcome: By accommodating tenant preferences and demonstrating flexibility in lease negotiations, the landlord secures a reputable tenant at favorable lease terms. The negotiated agreement reflects mutual understanding and addresses both landlord and tenant objectives, ensuring a stable rental income stream.

Chapter 7: **Building and Managing a Real Estate Portfolio**

Diversification is a fundamental strategy in real estate investing, aimed at reducing risk exposure and maximizing returns by spreading investments across various asset types, geographic locations, and investment strategies.

1. Property Types

Investing in diverse property types helps balance risk and return profiles within your portfolio:

Residential Properties: Single-family homes, condos, and apartment buildings cater to the residential rental market. They offer stable rental income and potential for appreciation, appealing to long-term investors seeking consistent cash flow.

Commercial Properties: Includes office buildings, retail spaces, and mixed-use developments. Commercial properties often generate higher rental yields but may involve longer lease terms and tenant turnover considerations.

Industrial Properties: Warehouses, distribution centers, and manufacturing facilities serve industrial tenants. These properties can provide steady rental income with lower maintenance costs compared to other commercial sectors.

Mixed-Use Properties: Combine residential, commercial, and retail spaces in a single development. Mixed-use properties offer diversification benefits by attracting different tenant types and revenue streams.

2. Geographic Diversification

Spread investments across diverse geographic locations to mitigate local market risks and capitalize on regional economic cycles:

City Diversification: Invest in properties across multiple cities within the same region or across different states to balance exposure to local economic conditions, employment trends, and demographic shifts.

International Investments: Consider expanding your portfolio internationally to access emerging markets or capitalize on global economic opportunities. International investments require thorough market research and understanding of local regulations.

3. Investment Strategies

Deploying various investment strategies can further diversify your real estate portfolio and enhance overall returns:

Buy-and-Hold Strategy: Acquire properties with the intention of holding them for long-term appreciation and rental income. Buy-and-hold strategies benefit from passive income streams, tax advantages such as depreciation, and potential equity growth over time.

Fix-and-Flip Strategy: Purchase distressed properties, renovate or improve them, and sell for a profit within a short timeframe. Fix-and-flip investments offer high potential returns but involve higher risks, requiring expertise in property rehabilitation and market timing.

Wholesaling: Facilitate property transactions as an intermediary without taking ownership. Wholesaling involves identifying distressed properties, negotiating contracts, and assigning them to buyers for a fee. It requires strong negotiation skills and a robust network of investors.

Long-Term vs. Short-Term Investments

Understanding the distinctions between long-term and short-term real estate investments is crucial for strategic portfolio management:

1. Long-Term Investments

Duration: Typically held for 5-10 years or more, focusing on sustainable growth and income generation.

Benefits:

Appreciation: Properties appreciate in value over time, increasing equity and net worth.
Rental Income: Stable cash flow from tenant rents provides consistent income streams.
Tax Advantages: Depreciation deductions and capital gains tax benefits enhance after-tax returns.
Risk Profile: Long-term investments are generally less volatile, benefiting from market stability and gradual property appreciation.

2. Short-Term Investments

Duration: Involves buying and selling properties within a shorter timeframe, typically within a year.

Strategies:

Fix-and-Flip: Purchase distressed properties, renovate them quickly, and sell at a higher price.
Development Projects: Participate in new construction or redevelopment projects aimed at quick turnaround and profit realization.
Benefits:

High Returns: Potential for quick profits through property value appreciation or resale margins.
Flexibility: Enables rapid capital turnover and reinvestment in new opportunities.
Risk Profile: Short-term investments are higher risk due to market volatility, construction delays, and market fluctuations impacting resale values.

Effective Portfolio Management Strategies

Managing a diversified real estate portfolio requires proactive oversight and strategic planning to optimize performance and mitigate risks:

1. Regular Portfolio Reviews

Performance Evaluation: Conduct periodic reviews to assess property performance, financial metrics, and overall portfolio health.

Asset Allocation: Adjust allocation based on market conditions, investment goals, and risk tolerance to optimize portfolio diversification and enhance returns.

2. Risk Management

Insurance Coverage: Maintain adequate property insurance coverage against natural disasters, liability claims, and tenant-related risks.

Emergency Funds: Set aside reserves for unforeseen expenses, such as property repairs, vacancies, or economic downturns impacting rental income.

3. Professional Property Management

Expert Oversight: Consider hiring professional property managers to handle day-to-day operations, tenant relations, maintenance, and lease agreements.

Strategic Guidance: Property managers provide market insights, rental market analysis, and cost-effective maintenance solutions to enhance property value and tenant satisfaction.

4. Technology and Tools

Portfolio Management Software: Utilize real estate investment platforms, financial analysis tools, and property management software to streamline operations, track performance metrics, and make data-driven decisions.

Market Insights: Access real-time market data, property comparables (comps), and investment trends to identify emerging opportunities and optimize portfolio allocation.

Chapter 8: Marketing Your Properties

Effective marketing is essential for attracting buyers or tenants and maximizing the value of your properties. By employing strategic approaches and leveraging digital tools, you can enhance property visibility, generate leads, and expedite successful transactions.

1. Enhancing Property Appeal

Enhancing the appeal of your property listings through visual presentation and compelling descriptions significantly impacts buyer or tenant interest:

Professional Photography:
High-quality photographs are instrumental in showcasing property features and attracting potential buyers or tenants. Consider hiring a professional photographer to capture well-lit, aesthetically pleasing images that highlight key selling points.

Staging:
Staging transforms a property into a desirable living space, enabling potential buyers or tenants to envision themselves residing there. Invest in professional staging services or utilize virtual staging tools to furnish and decorate vacant properties effectively.

Descriptive Listings:

Craft detailed and compelling property descriptions that emphasize unique features, amenities, and location benefits. Use clear, engaging language to convey property value and appeal to your target audience's preferences and needs.

2. Leveraging Digital Marketing Tools and Social Media

Digital marketing and social media platforms offer expansive reach and engagement opportunities for real estate marketing:

Real Estate Websites:
List your properties on prominent real estate websites such as Zillow, Realtor.com, and Redfin. These platforms attract a large audience of potential buyers and tenants actively searching for properties in specific locations.

Social Media Marketing:
Harness the power of social media platforms including Facebook, Instagram, and LinkedIn to promote your properties. Share visually appealing photos, engaging videos, and informative content about property features, local amenities, and market trends. Engage with followers, respond to inquiries promptly, and use targeted advertising to reach specific demographics.

Email Marketing:
Build an email list comprising potential buyers, tenants, and investors interested in real estate opportunities. Send regular newsletters featuring property updates, market insights, investment opportunities, and success stories. Personalize content to nurture leads and maintain client relationships over time.

3. Creating Compelling Property Listings

Crafting compelling property listings is crucial for capturing attention, generating interest, and prompting action from prospective buyers or tenants:

Catchy Headlines:
Use attention-grabbing headlines that highlight unique property features, desirable location benefits, or exclusive offers. Compelling headlines pique curiosity and encourage potential buyers or tenants to explore further.

Detailed Descriptions:

Provide comprehensive property descriptions that include key details such as property size, layout, architectural style, and notable amenities. Highlight recent upgrades, renovations, or energy-efficient features that add value and appeal to discerning buyers or tenants.

Call to Action (CTA):
Incorporate a clear and concise call to action in your property listings, prompting readers to take the next step. Examples include "Schedule a Viewing," "Request More Information," or "Contact Us Today." Ensure CTAs are prominently displayed and easy to follow, directing interested parties towards property tours or inquiries.

4. Monitoring and Optimizing Marketing Efforts

Continuously monitor the performance of your marketing campaigns and adjust strategies to optimize results:

Analytics and Metrics:
Utilize analytics tools provided by real estate websites, social media platforms, and email marketing services to track engagement metrics, website traffic, lead conversions, and campaign effectiveness. Analyze data to identify successful tactics, refine targeting strategies, and allocate marketing resources efficiently.

Feedback and Adaptation:
Solicit feedback from clients, prospects, and industry peers to gain insights into market preferences, customer satisfaction levels, and emerging trends. Use feedback to adapt marketing messages, enhance service offerings, and tailor promotional efforts to meet evolving market demands.

5. Compliance and Legal Considerations

Ensure compliance with real estate regulations, fair housing laws, and data privacy policies when conducting marketing activities. Adhere to ethical standards, maintain transparency in advertising practices, and protect client confidentiality to build trust and credibility within the real estate community and among prospective clients.

Chapter 9: **Legal and Regulatory Considerations**

In the intricate landscape of real estate investment, understanding and adhering to legal frameworks are paramount to success and risk management. Whether buying, selling, renting, or managing properties, comprehensive knowledge of applicable laws and regulations ensures compliance, mitigates risks, and safeguards investments. This guide delves into key legal areas every real estate investor should grasp.

1. Property Ownership Structures

Property ownership structures dictate legal rights, responsibilities, and implications:

Sole Ownership: Owned by a single individual, granting full control and decision-making authority over the property.

Joint Tenancy: Co-owned by two or more individuals with equal rights to the property. Joint tenancy includes rights of survivorship, meaning ownership transfers to surviving co-owners upon death.

Tenancy in Common: Co-ownership where each owner holds a distinct, undivided interest in the property. Unlike joint tenancy, there are no rights of survivorship; each owner can transfer their share independently.

Understanding these forms aids in choosing the most suitable ownership structure aligned with investment goals and estate planning needs.

2. Zoning and Land Use Regulations

Zoning laws govern how land and properties can be used within specific geographic areas:

Compliance Requirements: Verify that properties conform to local zoning ordinances dictating permissible land use, building size, and property type. Non-compliance can lead to fines, forced modifications, or legal disputes.

Variances and Special Use Permits: Obtain variances or special use permits for activities or developments not typically allowed under existing zoning regulations. Applications require demonstrating the project's adherence to community interests and zoning objectives.

Navigating zoning laws ensures projects align with municipal planning goals while mitigating legal challenges.

3. Tenant Laws and Lease Agreements

Tenant laws protect renters' rights and outline landlord obligations, critical for property management:

Lease Agreements: Formal contracts detailing rental terms, responsibilities, and rights of landlords and tenants. Include clauses on rent amounts, lease duration, maintenance duties, and rules governing property use.

Security Deposits: Regulations stipulate allowable deposit amounts, handling procedures, and conditions for withholding funds upon lease termination.
Eviction Procedures: Legal grounds and due process requirements for evicting tenants vary by jurisdiction. Compliance ensures lawful eviction proceedings while protecting tenant rights.
Adhering to tenant laws fosters positive landlord-tenant relationships and mitigates legal disputes.

4. Contracts and Agreements

Contracts are foundational in real estate transactions, delineating rights, obligations, and terms of agreements:

Purchase Agreements: Formal contracts specifying property sale terms, including purchase price, contingencies (e.g., inspections, financing), and closing dates. Clear, precise terms mitigate misunderstandings and facilitate smooth transactions.
Lease Agreements: Legal documents outlining rental terms and conditions between landlords and tenants. Clarity on rent payments, lease duration, maintenance responsibilities, and dispute resolution protocols ensures mutual understanding and compliance.
Partnership Agreements: Governing documents for joint real estate ventures, defining partners' roles, contributions, profit-sharing arrangements, and exit strategies. Clearly defined agreements prevent conflicts and protect investors' interests.
Thoroughly reviewing and understanding contractual obligations safeguards against legal disputes and ensures enforceability of agreements.

5. Mitigating Risks and Legal Pitfalls

Protecting investments involves proactive risk management and adherence to legal best practices:

Due Diligence: Rigorous property inspection, title review, and assessment of zoning compliance prior to purchase minimize risks of undisclosed issues or legal entanglements.
Insurance Coverage: Securing comprehensive insurance policies (e.g., property, liability, landlord) shields investors from financial losses due to unforeseen events such as natural disasters, accidents, or tenant disputes.
Legal Counsel: Engaging experienced real estate attorneys for contract review, legal guidance, and compliance oversight. Legal experts provide strategic advice, navigate complex legal scenarios, and safeguard investors' legal rights.
Collaborating with legal professionals ensures adherence to evolving regulations and safeguards long-term real estate investments.

Chapter 10: **Scaling Your Real Estate Business**

Scaling a real estate business involves expanding portfolios, optimizing operations, leveraging technology, building a capable team, and fostering a positive organizational culture. This comprehensive guide explores key strategies and best practices to effectively scale your real estate ventures.

1. Expand Your Portfolio

Expanding your portfolio is essential for scaling your real estate business:

Continuous Investment: Continuously seek new investment opportunities across different property types (residential, commercial, industrial) and geographic locations. Diversification reduces risk and enhances potential returns.
Strategic Acquisitions: Identify properties with growth potential, favorable market conditions, and alignment with your investment strategy (e.g., buy-and-hold, fix-and-flip). Conduct thorough due diligence to mitigate risks and maximize profitability.
Portfolio Management: Implement robust portfolio management practices to monitor property performance, optimize asset allocation, and capitalize on market opportunities.
2. Optimize Operations

Efficient operations are critical for scaling without compromising quality or increasing costs:

Standard Operating Procedures (SOPs): Develop and implement SOPs for property management, maintenance, tenant relations, and financial management. SOPs ensure consistency, streamline workflows, and enhance operational efficiency.
Technology Integration: Leverage property management software (e.g., Buildium, AppFolio, Rentec Direct) to automate routine tasks such as lease management, rent collection, maintenance tracking, and tenant communication. Automation reduces administrative burden and improves productivity.
Outsourcing Non-Core Activities: Consider outsourcing non-core functions such as accounting, legal services, and marketing to specialized professionals or firms. Outsourcing allows you to focus on core business activities and strategic growth initiatives.
3. Increase Revenue Streams

Diversifying revenue streams strengthens financial resilience and enhances overall business profitability:

Property Management Services: Offer property management services to external property owners or investors. Provide comprehensive management solutions including tenant screening, lease administration, maintenance coordination, and financial reporting.

Vacation Rentals and Short-Term Rentals: Explore opportunities in vacation rentals or short-term rental markets (e.g., Airbnb). These platforms offer higher rental yields but require careful management and compliance with local regulations.

Real Estate Development: Participate in real estate development projects to capitalize on value-add opportunities, redevelopment initiatives, or new construction projects. Development projects can generate substantial returns but involve higher risks and longer investment horizons.

4. Leveraging Technology and Automation

Technology enhances operational efficiency, data-driven decision-making, and customer service excellence:

Property Management Software: Utilize advanced property management software to streamline operations, enhance tenant satisfaction, and improve financial transparency. These platforms facilitate online rent payments, maintenance ticketing, and tenant portals for seamless communication.

Marketing Automation: Implement marketing automation tools (e.g., Mailchimp, HubSpot, Hootsuite) to automate lead generation, nurture client relationships, and track marketing performance. Schedule social media posts, email campaigns, and digital advertising to maximize reach and engagement.

Data Analytics: Harness the power of data analytics tools (e.g., REIPro, RealData, CoStar) to analyze market trends, assess property performance, and identify investment opportunities. Data-driven insights enable informed decision-making and proactive portfolio management.

5. Building a Team and Delegating Tasks

A capable and motivated team is instrumental in achieving sustainable growth and operational excellence:

Strategic Hiring: Recruit experienced professionals such as property managers, real estate agents, accountants, and legal advisors. Their expertise enhances operational efficiency, regulatory compliance, and strategic decision-making.

Delegation: Delegate tasks to team members based on their strengths and expertise. Empower employees to take ownership of responsibilities, foster innovation, and contribute to organizational success.

Positive Work Culture: Cultivate a positive work environment that promotes collaboration, innovation, and continuous learning. Encourage open communication, recognize achievements, and prioritize employee development to foster a motivated and engaged team.

Chapter 11: Real Estate Investment Strategies for Beginners

Real estate investing offers various strategies tailored to different investor goals, from generating passive income to achieving substantial returns through active management. This guide explores common investment strategies, case studies of successful beginner investors, and a step-by-step approach to making your first real estate investment.

1. Common Investment Strategies

Buy-and-Hold:
Buy-and-hold strategy involves purchasing properties with the intention of holding them for the long term to benefit from rental income and property appreciation. This strategy is favored by investors seeking steady cash flow and long-term wealth accumulation.

Fix-and-Flip:
Fix-and-flip strategy entails purchasing distressed properties at a discount, renovating them to increase their value, and selling them quickly for a profit. Successful execution requires a keen understanding of renovation costs, market trends, and efficient project management.

Wholesaling:
Wholesaling involves finding discounted properties, securing them under contract, and then assigning the contract to another buyer for a fee. This strategy requires strong negotiation skills, market knowledge, and a network of potential buyers.

2. Case Studies of Successful Beginner Investors

Case Study 1: The First Rental Property
A beginner investor purchases their first rental property—a duplex in a growing neighborhood. They secure a favorable loan, find reliable tenants, and achieve positive cash flow. Over time, the property appreciates, allowing the investor to leverage equity for additional investments.

Case Study 2: The Fix-and-Flip Success
A new investor identifies a distressed property in a desirable location. They purchase the property at a significant discount, manage renovations within budget and on schedule, and sell it for a substantial profit. The profits are reinvested into their next fix-and-flip project, accelerating their portfolio growth.

Case Study 3: The Wholesaling Journey
A beginner wholesaler negotiates a favorable contract with a motivated seller for a distressed property. They quickly find an interested buyer and assign the contract for a fee, generating immediate income. With repeat success, the wholesaler builds a reputation and establishes a steady stream of deals.

3. Step-by-Step Guide to Your First Investment

Set Clear Goals:
Define your investment objectives, whether it's passive income, wealth accumulation, or financial independence. Clear goals guide your investment strategy and decision-making process.

Educate Yourself:
Invest in real estate education by reading books, taking courses, and participating in local real estate groups. Understanding market dynamics, investment strategies, and legal considerations is crucial for informed decision-making.

Create a Budget:
Assess your financial situation and determine how much capital you can allocate to your first investment. Establish a budget that includes purchase costs, renovations (if applicable), and contingencies.

Research Markets:
Conduct thorough market research to identify areas with strong growth potential, favorable rental demand, and investment opportunities aligned with your goals. Analyze economic indicators, local market trends, and property appreciation rates.

Secure Financing:
Explore financing options such as conventional loans, FHA loans, or private money lenders. Get pre-approved for a loan to strengthen your position when making offers on properties. Build relationships with lenders to facilitate smoother transactions.

Find a Property:
Utilize online resources, real estate agents, and networking events to identify potential properties that meet your investment criteria. Perform due diligence by inspecting properties, reviewing financials, and assessing market comparables (comps).

Make an Offer:

Negotiate the purchase price and terms based on your research and budget. Be prepared to walk away if the deal doesn't align with your investment strategy or financial objectives.

Close the Deal:
Work with a real estate attorney to review contracts, ensure legal compliance, and complete the closing process smoothly. Address any contingencies or legal issues to finalize the transaction.

Manage the Property:
If investing in rental properties, find tenants through effective marketing strategies, screen applicants rigorously, and manage the property professionally. For fix-and-flip projects, oversee renovations to enhance property value and prepare for a profitable sale.

Reflect and Learn:
After completing your first investment, reflect on your experience, challenges faced, and lessons learned. Use these insights to refine your strategy, improve decision-making, and plan future investments effectively.

Chapter 12: **Advanced Real Estate Investment Strategies**

Advanced investors in real estate employ sophisticated techniques to maximize returns and manage risks effectively. This guide explores advanced strategies such as real estate syndication, 1031 exchanges, opportunity zones, as well as insights into real estate development and global investment opportunities.

1. Advanced Investment Strategies

Real Estate Syndication:
Real estate syndication involves pooling resources with other investors to collectively purchase larger properties, such as apartment complexes or commercial buildings. This strategy allows investors to access larger deals that might be beyond their individual financial capacity. Syndication spreads risks and rewards among multiple investors, providing opportunities for diversified investments and potentially higher returns.

1031 Exchanges:
A 1031 exchange, named after Section 1031 of the IRS tax code, enables investors to defer capital gains taxes by reinvesting proceeds from the sale of an investment property into a like-kind property. This strategy facilitates portfolio growth without immediate tax liabilities, allowing investors to reinvest gains into higher-value properties over time.

Opportunity Zones:
Investing in Opportunity Zones designated by the government offers tax benefits, including deferral, reduction, or elimination of capital gains taxes. These zones aim to spur economic development in distressed communities by incentivizing investment. Opportunity zone investments can provide attractive returns while contributing to community revitalization efforts.

2. Understanding Real Estate Development

Real estate development involves creating new properties or enhancing existing ones to increase their value. Successful real estate development requires comprehensive planning, financial acumen, and effective risk management.

Feasibility Studies:
Before embarking on a development project, conduct feasibility studies to assess its viability. This includes analyzing market demand, evaluating construction costs, understanding zoning regulations, and projecting potential returns. Feasibility studies help developers make informed decisions and mitigate risks associated with new developments.

Financing Development Projects:
Secure financing for development projects through various sources such as construction loans, joint ventures with investors, or private equity. Development projects typically require substantial capital and careful financial planning to cover construction costs, regulatory compliance, and potential contingencies.

Managing Development Risks:
Identify and manage risks inherent in development projects, such as construction delays, unexpected cost escalations, and fluctuations in market conditions. Collaborate with experienced contractors, architects, and project managers to implement risk mitigation strategies and ensure project success.

3. Global Real Estate Investment Opportunities

Investing internationally offers diversification benefits and access to potentially high-yielding markets. However, international real estate investments require thorough research, understanding of local regulations, and consideration of economic and political factors.

Research Foreign Markets:

Before investing in foreign markets, thoroughly research the economic stability, political landscape, and legal framework of the target country. Analyze market trends, property values, rental demand, and potential risks to make informed investment decisions.

Local Partnerships:
Partner with local real estate professionals such as agents, attorneys, and property managers who possess deep knowledge of the local market dynamics and regulatory environment. Local partnerships provide valuable insights, facilitate smoother transactions, and help navigate cultural and legal complexities.

Currency and Tax Considerations:
Consider currency exchange rates and tax implications associated with international investments. Fluctuations in currency values can impact investment returns, while varying tax regulations may affect profitability and compliance requirements. Consult with tax advisors and legal experts to understand these considerations thoroughly.

Chapter 13: **Wealth Building and Financial Independence**

Creating multiple passive income streams through real estate is a strategic approach to achieving financial independence. This guide outlines various methods to generate passive income, strategies for long-term wealth building, and a roadmap to attain financial independence through real estate.

Creating Passive Income Streams in Real Estate
1. Rental Properties:
Investing in rental properties, whether residential or commercial, is a classic method to generate passive income. Rental income provides a steady cash flow while properties appreciate over time, building equity and wealth.

2. Real Estate Investment Trusts (REITs):
REITs offer investors an opportunity to gain exposure to real estate assets without owning physical properties. These trusts pool funds from multiple investors to invest in income-producing properties. REITs typically distribute a significant portion of their income as dividends, providing passive income to investors.

3. Crowdfunding Platforms:
Real estate crowdfunding platforms, such as Fundrise and RealtyMogul, enable investors to participate in real estate projects with lower capital requirements. These platforms pool funds

from individual investors to finance a variety of real estate ventures, offering returns through rental income, property appreciation, or profit sharing.

Strategies for Long-Term Wealth Building
Building sustainable wealth through real estate involves strategic planning and disciplined execution of investment strategies.

1. Reinvestment:
Reinvesting profits and rental income into additional properties can accelerate wealth growth through compounding. By continuously acquiring new properties, investors increase their passive income streams and benefit from portfolio diversification.

2. Leverage:
Utilizing leverage, such as mortgage financing, allows investors to control more assets with less upfront capital. While leverage amplifies returns, it's essential to manage debt carefully to avoid overexposure to risk.

3. Tax Optimization:
Maximizing tax benefits is crucial for enhancing real estate investment returns. Strategies like depreciation deductions, 1031 exchanges for deferring capital gains taxes, and investments in Opportunity Zones for tax incentives can significantly reduce tax liabilities and increase cash flow.

Achieving Financial Independence Through Real Estate
Financial independence, achieved through passive income that covers living expenses, is a goal many real estate investors aspire to attain.

1. Set Financial Goals:
Define clear financial independence goals, such as generating enough passive income to cover living expenses or achieving a specific net worth milestone.

2. Create a Plan:
Develop a detailed plan outlining how you will acquire properties, finance investments, and generate passive income. Consider factors like property location, market conditions, and investment timelines.

3. Build Passive Income:

Focus on acquiring properties that generate consistent passive income through rental payments. Aim for properties with positive cash flow and high occupancy rates to ensure reliable income streams.

4. Reduce Debt:

Paying down high-interest debt, particularly non-mortgage debt, improves financial stability and reduces financial risks associated with real estate investments.

5. Monitor Progress:

Regularly review your financial situation, track income, expenses, and net worth. Adjust your investment strategy as needed based on market conditions and personal financial goals.

6. Maintain a Growth Mindset:

Continuously educate yourself about real estate investing, stay informed about market trends, and explore new opportunities for growth and diversification within your portfolio.

Chapter 14: **Case Studies of Successful Investors**

Case Study 1: From Zero to Millionaire

Background: An aspiring investor starts their journey with a small single-family rental property in a growing suburban area. They begin modestly, managing the property themselves to learn the ropes of property management and tenant relations.

Strategies and Actions:

1. **Strategic Acquisitions:** As their initial property generates positive cash flow, they reinvest profits into acquiring additional rental properties. They focus on properties with potential for appreciation and steady rental income.
2. **Leveraging Partnerships:** Recognizing the limitations of personal capital, the investor partners with other like-minded individuals or institutions to finance larger acquisitions. This allows them to scale their portfolio more rapidly than would have been possible alone.
3. **Diversification:** Over time, they diversify their portfolio to include multi-family units, commercial properties, and even venture into development projects. Diversification helps spread risk and enhances overall portfolio stability.
4. **Long-Term Vision:** With a focus on long-term wealth building, the investor strategically holds onto properties, benefiting from both rental income and property appreciation over several market cycles.

Outcome: Over a decade of disciplined investing, strategic partnerships, and continuous reinvestment, the investor achieves a substantial net worth exceeding $10 million. Their diversified portfolio not only provides financial security but also positions them as a prominent player in the local real estate market.

Case Study 2: The Power of 1031 Exchanges

Background: Starting with a small rental property, this investor recognizes the potential of 1031 exchanges as a tax-deferral strategy to accelerate portfolio growth.

Strategies and Actions:

1. **Initial Investment:** They begin with a single rental property, focusing on properties with potential for capital appreciation and consistent rental income.
2. **Using 1031 Exchanges:** After gaining equity in their initial property, they sell it and reinvest the proceeds into a larger, more lucrative property through a 1031 exchange. This allows them to defer capital gains taxes and leverage their gains into a larger investment.
3. **Reinvestment Strategy:** Continually leveraging 1031 exchanges, they repeat the process, upgrading to larger properties or diversifying into different asset classes. Each exchange fuels portfolio expansion without immediate tax liabilities, maximizing returns on invested capital.
4. **Strategic Timing:** They carefully time their exchanges to align with market cycles and investment opportunities, ensuring optimal growth and minimizing risks.

Outcome: By systematically reinvesting profits and utilizing 1031 exchanges, the investor significantly scales their portfolio over a relatively short period. They accumulate wealth through property appreciation and rental income while deferring substantial tax liabilities, setting a solid foundation for long-term financial success.

Case Study 3: Investing in Opportunity Zones

Background: An investor with a keen eye for emerging markets and tax incentives identifies Opportunity Zones as a promising investment opportunity.

Strategies and Actions:

1. **Market Research:** They conduct thorough market research to identify distressed properties in Opportunity Zones with potential for revitalization and future appreciation.
2. **Property Improvement:** By acquiring undervalued properties, they implement strategic renovations and improvements to enhance property value and attract tenants or buyers.

3. **Capitalizing on Tax Incentives:** Taking advantage of Opportunity Zone tax benefits, including capital gains deferral, reduction, or elimination, they maximize investment returns while contributing to community development.
4. **Risk Management:** Despite the potential for higher returns, they mitigate risks through meticulous due diligence, strategic planning, and leveraging professional expertise in property development and finance.

Outcome: Through strategic investments in Opportunity Zones, the investor achieves impressive returns while making a positive impact on local communities. Their success underscores the importance of proactive market analysis, effective use of tax incentives, and prudent risk management in real estate investing.

Analyzing Key Factors in Their Success

1. Strategic Planning

Successful investors begin with clear goals and develop well-defined plans tailored to their financial objectives and risk tolerance. They conduct comprehensive market analyses, assess property performance metrics, and outline achievable milestones.

2. Continuous Learning

Investors commit to continuous education and stay informed about evolving industry trends, market dynamics, and regulatory changes. They leverage resources such as industry publications, seminars, and networking events to refine their investment strategies and adapt to market fluctuations.

3. Networking

Building robust networks with industry professionals, mentors, and fellow investors provides valuable insights, support, and access to investment opportunities. Successful investors cultivate relationships that foster collaboration, knowledge sharing, and potential partnerships for mutual benefit.

4. Resilience and Adaptability

Navigating the complexities of real estate investing requires resilience in overcoming setbacks and adapting strategies to changing market conditions. Successful investors learn from failures, adjust their approaches, and maintain focus on long-term goals amidst economic uncertainties.

Chapter 15: Your Roadmap to Real Estate Success

Real estate investing offers numerous opportunities for wealth creation and financial independence. Success in this field requires a combination of mindset, knowledge, strategic action, and resilience. Here's how to put it all together to create your personalized action plan.

1. Mindset: Cultivating Success
Growth Mindset: Adopt a growth mindset that embraces challenges, sees failures as learning opportunities, and believes in continuous improvement. Overcome mental barriers such as fear of failure or uncertainty by focusing on your goals and staying resilient.

Resilience and Adaptability: Real estate investing can be unpredictable. Develop resilience to bounce back from setbacks and adaptability to adjust strategies in response to market changes or unexpected challenges.

2. Knowledge: Continuous Learning and Networking
Continuous Education: Invest time in expanding your knowledge of real estate investing. Read books, attend seminars, take online courses, and participate in local real estate groups. Stay informed about market trends, legal regulations, and best practices.

Building a Network: Networking is crucial. Build relationships with mentors, peers, real estate agents, lenders, and other industry professionals. Networking provides insights, support, and potential partnership opportunities.

3. Action: Creating Your Personalized Action Plan
Set Clear Goals: Define your real estate investment goals. Whether it's generating passive income through rental properties, building long-term wealth, or achieving financial independence, clarity in goals is essential for strategic planning.

Research and Educate: Conduct thorough research on different real estate markets. Analyze economic indicators, local demographics, rental trends, and property values. Educate yourself on financing options, including mortgages, loans, and alternative funding sources.

Create a Budget: Determine your investment budget and explore financing options. Build relationships with lenders and secure pre-approval for loans to expedite the purchasing process when opportunities arise.

Identify Opportunities: Use your research to identify promising investment opportunities. Look for properties with potential for appreciation, strong rental demand, or value-add opportunities through renovations or repositioning.

Take Action: Once you've identified opportunities, take decisive action. Make offers, negotiate deals, and execute transactions. Start with manageable investments and gradually scale your portfolio as you gain experience and confidence.

Manage and Grow: Effective property management is crucial. Implement systems for tenant screening, rent collection, maintenance, and financial reporting. Continuously optimize operations to maximize cash flow and property value.

4. Staying Motivated and Adapting to Challenges
Set Milestones: Break down your goals into smaller, achievable milestones. Celebrate each milestone reached, as it reinforces your progress and motivates further action.

Stay Flexible: The real estate market is dynamic and subject to fluctuations. Be flexible in adapting your strategies to changing market conditions, economic shifts, or unexpected events.

Seek Support: Surround yourself with a supportive network of mentors, peers, and professionals. Seek advice, share experiences, and learn from others' successes and challenges in real estate investing.

Maintain Positivity: Stay positive and focused on your goals. Real estate investing can be demanding, but maintaining a positive outlook will help you navigate obstacles and setbacks effectively.

Chapter 16: Conclusion: Embarking on Your Real Estate Journey

Congratulations on completing this comprehensive guide to real estate investing! Throughout this book, we've explored the essential elements of success in real estate, from mastering the mindset of a successful investor to navigating complex strategies and market dynamics.

Reflecting on Your Journey
As you reflect on the wealth of information and strategies presented, remember that real estate investing is both an art and a science. It requires not only knowledge and strategic planning but also adaptability, resilience, and a proactive approach to seizing opportunities.

Embracing a Growth Mindset

Central to your success will be cultivating a growth mindset—an outlook that embraces challenges, learns from setbacks, and continuously seeks improvement. Your journey in real estate investing will undoubtedly present hurdles, but with the right mindset, each challenge becomes an opportunity for growth and learning.

Building on Knowledge and Networks
Investing in real estate demands a commitment to ongoing education and networking. Stay informed about market trends, legal developments, and best practices. Build a robust network of mentors, peers, and industry professionals whose insights and support will be invaluable as you navigate the complexities of real estate transactions.

Crafting Your Personal Action Plan
Armed with the knowledge gained from this book, create a personalized action plan tailored to your investment goals. Define clear objectives, research diligently, and take decisive action when opportunities arise. Remember to set achievable milestones, celebrate your successes, and adjust your strategies as needed to stay on course towards financial independence.

Maintaining Resilience and Positivity
Above all, maintain resilience and positivity throughout your real estate journey. The path to success may involve setbacks and challenges, but perseverance and a positive outlook will see you through. Surround yourself with a supportive network, seek guidance when needed, and trust in your ability to overcome obstacles on the path to achieving your financial goals.

Moving Forward
Now equipped with the tools, strategies, and mindset of a successful real estate investor, you are poised to embark on your journey towards building wealth and achieving financial independence through real estate. Stay committed, stay focused, and embrace the opportunities that lie ahead.

Your Real Estate Journey Begins Now!
As you close this book, remember that your journey in real estate investing is just beginning. Each step you take, informed by the principles and insights shared here, brings you closer to realizing your dreams of financial freedom and long-term prosperity.

Go forth with confidence, courage, and a commitment to excellence in all your real estate endeavors. Your future as a successful real estate investor awaits—start building it today!

www.ingramcontent.com/pod-product-compliance
Lightning Source LLC
Chambersburg PA
CBHW072056230526
45479CB00010B/1098